AN APPLE A DAY!

by Jennifer Storey Gillis

Illustrated by Patti Delmonte

A TRUMPET CLUB SPECIAL EDITION

Edited by Gwen W. Steege
Design by Carol J. Jessop

Published by The Trumpet Club, Inc.,
a subsidiary of Bantam Doubleday Dell Publishing Group, Inc.,
1540 Broadway, New York, New York 10036.
"A Trumpet Club Special Edition" with the portrayal
of a trumpet and two circles is a registered trademark of
Bantam Doubleday Dell Publishing Group, Inc.

ISBN 0-440-83403-1

This edition published by arrangement with
Storey Communications, Inc.
Printed in the United States of America
May 1995   RRC   10 9 8 7 6 5 4 3 2 1

Some recipes in this book are adapted from recipes in other books
from Storey Communications, Inc.: page 18, from *Let's Grow!*, by
Linda Tilgner; pages 38, 40, 44, and 50 from *The Apple Cookbook*, by
Olwen Woodier; page 54 from *Food to Grow On*, by Nancy Van
Leuven. All titles are available through Storey Communications,
Inc., Schoolhouse Road, Pownal, Vermont 05261 (1-800-441-5700).

Table of Contents

Tools of the Trade

Whether you are using apples for an arts-and-crafts project or for a recipe, here are some simple terms that will be helpful for you to learn. Here are some tools, too, that are useful for cutting apples. All can be found in kitchen stores or hardware stores near you.

Peel. This one is easy. It means to take the skin off of the apple! Get a grown-up helper to use a sharp paring knife to carefully take off the skin. Remember, however, that many of an apple's vitamins are in its skin — and so is its sweet smell — so don't  think you always need to peel an apple, unless a recipe requires it.

Core. This means to take out the middle of the apple without cutting the whole apple up into pieces.

Slice. This means to cut into a number of pieces. Let your grown-up helper do any cutting that is needed.

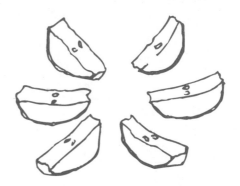

down. After you pull the corer back out, you should be able to push the core out with your fingers and have an apple with a hole right through its middle!

Apple Corer-Slicer. This hand-held tool slices *and* cores your apple! Put your apple on a cutting board. Hold the corer-slicer with two hands and push it down over the apple. You should end up with the core taken out and eight slices of apple — all with one push!

Apple Corer. This hand-held kitchen tool lets you easily core an apple. If your grown-up helper gets you started, you can core an apple this way. Insert the tool around the stem of the apple, and carefully push it straight

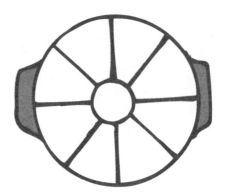

2

Apple Corer-Peeler-Slicer. The very neatest of all, this is a tool that you attach to your kitchen counter and it does all three of these jobs. The apple goes on the spear, and then all you do is crank the handle. A long, thin strip of apple peel comes off and the core is taken out while a blade cuts the apples into rings. You are left with an apple that is ready to go right into the pie! (You can eat the long strip of apple skin that comes off!)

The flower — apple blossom — is the part of the tree that grows into an apple!

blossom

young fruit

mature apples

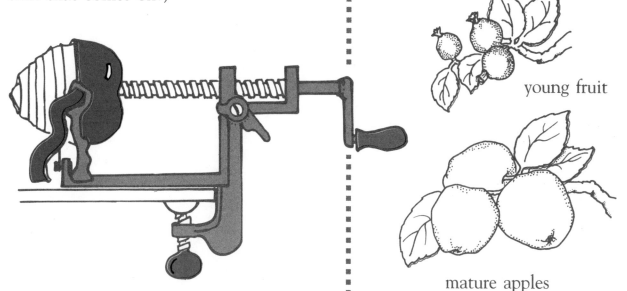

Be an Apple Expert

There's more to an apple than meets the eye!
With hundreds of kinds to choose from, the
apple experts must know the right
apple for each project.
Fall is the best time for picking your own
apples, but one of the wonderful things about
apples is that they are available for projects and
recipes all year long. Read the following few
pages, and you may learn enough to be
the next Johnny Appleseed!

Apple Cultivars

Apples come in hundreds of sizes, shapes, and even colors! The different kinds are called **cultivars** or **varieties,** and each one has a name. Each has a unique taste as well, and the apple expert will tell you that the perfect apple for a pie is *not* the same as the perfect lunchbox apple!

Best Lunchbox Apples

Empire
McIntosh
Paulared

Best Pie Apple
Northern Spy

The most common apple varieties in the United States are McIntosh, Red Delicious, Golden Delicious, and Granny Smith. But these are only a few of the wonderful varieties that are available. Try a Paulared, an Empire, or a Northern Spy!

Winter Banana

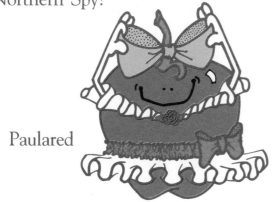

Paulared

Some unusual apple varieties include the Summer Rambo, Sheepnose, Winter Banana, and Cox's Orange Pippin. Can you imagine what these apples look like? Use your imagination and draw these funny apples!

Northern Spy

Sheepnose

An Apple a Day
Keeps the Doctor Away

 What does it mean to say "An Apple a Day Keeps the Doctor Away"? If you eat one apple every day will you *really* keep the doctor away? No, but apples *are* very healthful snacks — better for you than you may know.

 Apples are great for quenching your thirst, because they are made up mostly of water. Try one when you are thirsty and see how it works.

 Apples are terrific teeth cleaners and teeth strengtheners. Notice how shiny and clean your teeth feel when you finish eating an apple.

 Apples are full of many important vitamins, including vitamins A, B, and C.

Apple skin consists of fiber, which your body needs every day.

 Best of all, apples taste great! I'll take an apple "vitamin" any day!

What Is a Metaphor?

A metaphor is a special way of comparing two very different things by using words or phrases to suggest similarities between the two. One example is: "He was drowning in money." Of course, this doesn't mean he was really drowning. It means that he had so much money he didn't know what to do with it all!

"She is the apple of my eye" is another metaphor. This one means that she is what brings me happiness or joy. There aren't really any apples under my lids!

Can you think of any other metaphors having to do with apples? (See Answer Page.)

Apple Geography

Apples are grown in many areas of the world. They grow best in areas with winters that are moderately cool and summers that have sunny, warm days and cool nights. The best apple-growing states in the United States are California, Michigan, New York, North Carolina, Pennsylvania, Virginia, and Washington. Can you find all of them on a map? Are they all in the same area of the country? Do they have anything in common?

A standard apple tree lives an average of 100 years.

How Did Apples Get All over the World?

A man named John Chapman, who was born in Massachusetts in 1774, wanted to follow the pioneers out West. As he travelled, he *sowed* (planted) his apple seeds all along the way and became known as Johnny Appleseed. He is the most famous apple grower of all times, but certainly not the only one!

A sea captain carried an apple seed all the way from England to the state of Washington in 1826 and planted it. The tree is still growing today!

Granny Smith apples came all the way from Australia.

Apple Puzzle

Use your knowledge of apple growing states to finish this puzzle.

Across

3. State with the name of a former U.S. President
6. Not only apples, but movie stars grow here
7. Another state has a similar name, but it begins with South

Down

1. Many cars are made here
2. On the East Coast of the U.S.
4. Where the Empire State Building lives
5. Where they make Hershey's Chocolate Kisses

Answers on page 60.

11

Perfect Apple-Picking Picnic

*If you are lucky enough to live near an apple orchard that welcomes
visitors to picnic and pick your own apples, treat yourself to an
apple-picking picnic when autumn rolls around. Choose a beautiful day,
round up some friends and your family, and head off to the orchards!*

···WHAT YOU WILL NEED···

- ▶ Picnic basket
- ▶ Lunchtime goodies
- ▶ Cloth bags for picking apples
- ▶ Socks, shoes, and long pants
- ▶ Blanket

Poison ivy loves the shade of the apple trees as much as you do! It's best to wear shoes and socks and long pants — even on a warm, fall day. If you see a low-growing, green plant with shiny, rosy red leaves arranged in groups of three, you have probably found some poison ivy. Stay away — it's hard to eat an apple and scratch at the same time!

Watch out for bees! They love the sweet smell of the orchard. If you know you are allergic to bees, bring your bee sting kit along with you. If you are on a class trip, make sure to tell your teachers before you leave the school so that they can keep a special eye on you!

Pack a special picnic with a sandwich and a drink, but don't waste your time packing a dessert. You will be eating lots of sweet apples all day long.

Have a terrific time! Discover that the reddest apples aren't always the best and pick all different types of apples.

Clean up everything you brought with you to the orchard. You don't want to leave a trace of your picnic behind. If you find someone else's garbage, pick that up, too.

If you're lucky to find an orchard that makes its own cider — and maybe even cider doughnuts — sample some of each.

Storing and Saving Apples

If you want to save some of fall's freshest apples,
you'll need to learn a few techniques.

Cold Storage

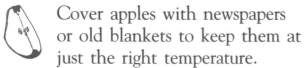 Make sure your apples are clean and dry. Wrap them in plastic bags with breathing holes (they don't really breathe, but they do like good air circulation).

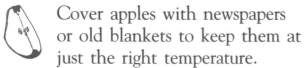 Cover apples with newspapers or old blankets to keep them at just the right temperature. They like nice, cold places — ideally between 32°–40°F. Keep some in your refrigerator, and some in your cellar or garage, if they are not too warm or too cold. Just be sure those little guys don't freeze!

Don't store your apples near your potatoes. The gasses an apple releases make the potatoes sprout too early.

 Check your apples every now and then, and take out any rotten or mushy ones. There's a saying that "One rotten apple spoils the whole bunch," and it's true. Get rid of those troublemakers early!

The apple skin is what makes the apple smell sweet.

Freezing Apples

Be sure to label and date all your frozen foods — an unmarked package will soon be forgotten in the back of the freezer!

1. With your grown-up helper, peel, core, and cut ten medium apples into ¼-inch slices. Drop them into Lemon Water (see recipe on page 17) for 5 minutes, so they don't turn brown.

2. Sprinkle extra-fine sugar over the bottom of a baking sheet. Layer the apple slices on top of the sugar. Sprinkle the apples with more sugar, then layer more apples. Repeat these layers until all of the slices have been lightly sweetened.

3. Put the apples and sugar from the pan into plastic freezer containers. Make sure you leave a little space (½-inch), because the apples will expand as they freeze. Cover them tightly and put them in the freezer. Use them for pies and cakes and other baking recipes. Enjoy a taste of fall all year long!

Lemon Water

Drop apples into the following mixture for 2 or 3 minutes to keep them from turning brown:

1 gallon cold water
2 tablespoons lemon juice

Freezing Pies

If you want to freeze an apple pie (recipe on page 38), here are a few things to keep in mind:

 Don't cut any air vents in the crust, until you are ready to bake the pie.

 Wrap your *unbaked* pie very well, first in plastic wrap and then in aluminum foil, to keep out the air.

Take the pie out of the freezer, and put it in a 425°F oven for 30 minutes. Turn the oven down to 350°F, and bake the pie for another 30 minutes.

 Dish out some vanilla ice cream and enjoy — any time of the year!

Drying Apples

1. Wash and dry as many apples as you have. Core them, and then ask for grown-up help to slice them into rings ¼ inch thick.

2. Thread the apple rings on a string, and hang them up in an airy, dry place. Cover them with cheesecloth to keep them clean.

3. When the apples are fully dry, pack them up in containers and cover the containers tightly. Use the apples for baking, or eat them as a snack.

Wear a string of dried apples as a necklace, and you have a traveling snack!

Tie a red or green ribbon around each dried slice, and hang a few on your Christmas tree as ornaments!

Microwave Drying

- 2 apples
- Lemon Water (page 17)
- Paper towels
- Microwave oven
- Kitchen paper
- Airtight containers

1. Peel and core the apples with your grown-up helper.

2. Cut each one into ten rings, about ¼ inch thick.

3. Soak them in Lemon Water, so they do not brown.

4. Drain the rings and pat them dry with paper towels.

5. Arrange the rings on a piece of kitchen paper, so they are not touching.

6. Put them in a microwave, and set on Defrost for 35–45 minutes. The apples will be rubbery and dry when they're done.

7. Store the rings in airtight containers and enjoy all year round!

The first apple orchard in North America was planted in Boston, Massachusetts, in 1625.

Growing Apple Mint

You can buy apple mint at a nursery or greenhouse, or perhaps a friend has some and will give you a snip. Use this apple mint the way you would use any mint — in your iced tea or lemonade, even in your salads. Plant this hardy mint where you have plenty of room, because it will grow and grow and grow!

··· WHAT YOU WILL NEED ···

- A well-drained, sunny area of the garden
- A trowel
- Peat moss or compost
- An apple mint plant
- Water

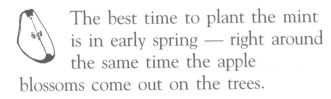 The best time to plant the mint is in early spring — right around the same time the apple blossoms come out on the trees.

Ask for a little section of your family's garden, but make sure they know your mint will spread! Spread some fertilizer or compost on the soil and dig it in, to make the soil healthy and rich.

 Dig a hole just the right size to hold the apple mint plant and the soil with it. The same amount of plant should show above the garden soil as shows above the soil in the pot. Press the soil around the plant firmly, and water well.

Over the next few weeks, pull any weeds that come up. Make sure to water the apple mint plant well. By the middle of the summer, you should have plenty of apple mint.

How Can You Tell This Is Mint?

◆ Rub the leaves between your fingers to release the fragrant oil of the plant. You'll recognize the nice, minty smell.

◆ All plants in the Mint Family have square stems! Cut a stem crosswise and notice the square corners.

Apple-Mint Tea

Take the stems you cut off your apple mint plant, wash them carefully, and lay them on a window screen or towel in a shady spot that gets lots of air — a porch is a good place. When they are dry, tie 4 or 5 stems together with string, and hang them upside down on a clothes-drying rack until the leaves are completely dry and crisp. Rub the dried leaves off the stems, and put the leaves in a jar with a tight-fitting lid.

When you want a cup of apple-mint tea, put about 1 teaspoonful of dried leaves in a tea strainer in a teacup, and pour a cup of boiling water over it. Add some lemon and honey, and enjoy! Apple-mint tea tastes great iced, too.

When your plant gets big and bushy, snip the stalks almost to the ground and get ready for a surprise! Strong, new leaves will grow back, better than ever.

Harvest your apple mint to use for making Apple-Mint Tea (see box at the left) or Apple-Mint Vinegar — an easy craft you can give as a gift to your friends and teachers! (See page 56 for the recipe.)

Any mature apple that is less than 2 inches in diameter can be called a crab apple.

Be an Apple Artist

Apples can be the centerpiece for many art activities — some of which you can make to hang on the 'fridge, others you can give away as gifts, and a few you can even eat!
Use these ideas as a guide for your own imagination. Remember, beauty is in the eye of the beholder. In other words, if you think it's fun to make and beautiful to look at, then it is truly art!

Apple-Head Clown Dolls

These happy clowns can be as simple or complicated as you like. Use toothpicks to stick on the decorations, or make it even easier and use peanut butter. Be prepared for messy (but quite happy) fingers! When your clown doll is all done, you can eat it right away, or set it aside and watch the clown face change a little each day as it dries.

WHAT YOU WILL NEED

- A large apple
- Paper plate
- Toothpicks
- Miniature marshmallows
- Raisins
- Peanut butter
- Sugar ice cream cone

1 Wash and dry a big apple. Place it on a paper plate in front of you. Figure out a game plan for creating a clown face. You know — do you want a happy face or a sad face? Sleepy or excited?

2 Using toothpicks to anchor the pieces, create a food face. Miniature marshmallows make great eyes, and raisins, a smiley mouth. Be creative and do whatever you want!

◆ After dipping the edge of the cone in peanut butter, dip it in chocolate or rainbow sprinkles.

◆ Anything you can stick a toothpick through can decorate an apple head. Try frozen banana slices, Lifesaver candies, and Cheerios!

◆ Make several different clown heads and you will have an entire apple-head circus!

3 Carefully dip the open end of the ice cream cone into some peanut butter. The peanut butter is the glue that will stick this cone hat to your apple head. If you'd like, you can use peanut butter to stick more raisins or sprinkles to the hat.

Apple Wreath

You can make these beautiful wreaths any time of the year,
but they are especially nice around the holidays.

apples, and make sure you leave the skins on!

 3 Soak the apples in Lemon Water.

 4 Poke the threaded needle through the center of each apple, until all the apples are strung on the thread. Hang them in an airy, dry place until they are dry, or dry them in a microwave oven (see page 19). When they are dry, read on.

 1 Wash and dry the five apples.

 2 Ask for help to cut the apples into ¼-inch-thick slices. Do not core the

 5 Draw a circle on your cardboard. It should measure about 10 to 12 inches in diameter (across the middle). Trace around a dinner plate, if you wish.

Draw a smaller circle in the middle, about 5 inches in diameter.

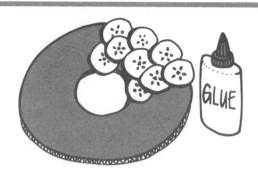

 Using your scissors, carefully cut out the little circle and then the big circle. You should have what looks like a giant Lifesaver made out of cardboard.

 Tie a ribbon through the middle and around the wreath so that you can hang it up. (But keep it in a flat position until the glue is thoroughly dry.)

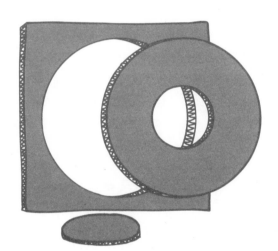

 The slightly red color of the dried apple skin adds a rosy glow to your wreath. If you want to add a few more decorations, try small pine cones, pine branches, or holly berries.

 Take your dried apple slices and glue them in a circle around the cardboard. Let them overlap so that very little of the cardboard shows through.

Apple Games

These games are great fun — especially in the fall when apples are plentiful.

Bobbing for Apples

A great Halloween party game! The winner is the one who gets the first apple,
or when you get really good at this, the one who gets the most apples!

•• WHAT YOU WILL NEED ••

▶ Large barrel or metal tub
▶ Clean water
▶ 1 dozen apples
▶ Towels for drying off
▶ Friends!

3 You and your friends kneel next to the barrel, put your hands behind your backs, and pick up the apples with your teeth! Easy, right?

1 Fill your barrel or tub with water. If it is a nice day, do this outside!

2 Place all the apples in the water — see how they float?

Juggling with Apples

This is easiest for those who can already juggle and are now looking for a challenge! If you are left handed, reverse all of the directions below. It is very hard to read directions for juggling. The best way to learn is to watch someone do it, and then practice on your own.

WHAT YOU WILL NEED

- 3 apples
- Patience!

1 Start by practicing with two apples. Put them both in your right hand and try to throw one up while the other rests in your hand. Now, throw the other one up while the first one comes down. If you can do this a few times, you can juggle!

2 Put the third apple in your left hand. Toss apple #1 up, then apple #2 up. While you catch #1 in your left hand, throw #3 up so you can catch #2 in your left hand. Keep this pattern up and you are juggling!

Be very patient — this is supposed to be fun, remember?!

29

Apple Toss

Getting the board ready takes some time and grown-up help, but when it's done, it's very easy for kids to drag this game out of the garage and play with it on their own.

WHAT YOU WILL NEED

- Large piece of plywood, about 4' x 4' x ¼"
- Jig saw or coping saw, for grown-up
- Paint and brushes
- 3 apples

"10" next to one hole, "20" next to another, and so on until each hole has a number. These numbers will help you keep score.

 Ask your grown-up helper to cut five holes in the board. They should be about 10 inches in diameter — big enough for an apple to sail through easily.

 Paint your board! Paint a circle around each hole, like a bull's-eye. Put the number

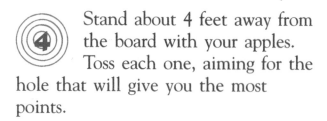 When the board is dry, prop it up against a tree or the garage door. You are ready to play!

Stand about 4 feet away from the board with your apples. Toss each one, aiming for the hole that will give you the most points.

 After all the players get a turn, add up the scores. When the game gets too easy, stand farther away to toss the apples.

6 Put the board away, so that you know where it is the next time you want to play!

Games are meant to be fun!
No one likes to play
with a sore loser.

Apple Prints

Print on plain-colored gift-wrapping paper to wrap your own presents.
Put on your smock and you're ready to go!

WHAT YOU WILL NEED

- 3 large apples
- Knife
- 6 colors of finger or tempera paints
- 6 paper plates or pie tins
- Newspaper
- Colored construction paper
- Smock

 3 Pour a different color paint onto each paper plate. Spread out the newspapers over your work table and place a piece of colored construction paper on top.

 4 Carefully dip the flat surface (the design) into the paint, and then press it on the paper.

 1 Get your grown-up helper to cut each apple in half crosswise.

2 Get a grown-up to help you cut a design on the flat surface. In the examples on the next page, the shaded areas are removed; the flat raised areas will print.

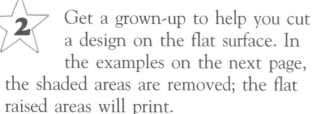

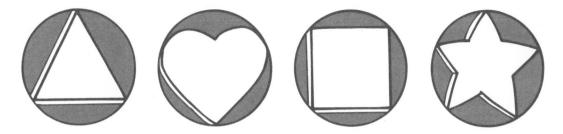

5 Remember to clean up your work space thoroughly. Throw out the paper plates, put the apples into the compost or garbage, recycle the newspapers, and wash your hands. By the time you are done, your pictures should be dry!

Printmaking Tips

◆ You will get the best results if you use one apple for each color. Once you start mixing paints, they each turn gray!

◆ The paint may make the apples slippery and hard to hold onto. Try using corn-on-the-cob holders to get a better grip.

Apple Stars

When you cut any apple in half horizontally, you will find an apple "star" inside. The way the seeds sit in the apple makes a five-pointed star. A fully developed apple has ten seeds inside. Count how many your apple has. If you cut the apple in half the *other* way (lengthwise), do you still see the star?

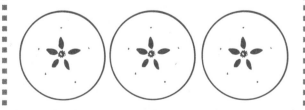

Applesauce Play Dough Jewelry

Here's a craft that smells so good you want to eat it,
but hang these lovely designs around your neck instead.

WHAT YOU WILL NEED

- ¼ cup ground cinnamon
- 2 tablespoons applesauce
- Small bowl and teaspoon
- Rolling pin
- Small cookie cutters and/or butter knife
- Toothpick
- Yarn or narrow ribbon, pin fasteners, glue

1. Mix the cinnamon and applesauce together in a small bowl. Add more cinnamon, if necessary, to make a non-sticky dough that you can model and roll.

2. Place the play dough on a clean surface and roll out with a rolling pin until the dough is about ¼ inch thick.

3. Cut out shapes with your cookie cutters, or cut out your own designs with a butter knife. With the toothpick, poke a small hole in the top of each cutout.

4. Place the cutouts on a paper towel on a microwave-safe plate. Microwave on High for 1 minute. Turn cutouts over and microwave for 30 seconds or until hardened. Allow cutouts to cool completely before you handle them. (You can also let them air dry naturally. It will take about two days.)

5. Cut a piece of yarn or narrow ribbon long enough to go around your neck. Thread the yarn through the hole in your cutout to make a pendant. Or, glue the cutout to a pin fastening. Now, you have a lovely, sweet-smelling pin to wear all year-round!

Cinnamon-Apple Beads

Instead of rolling the play dough out flat, use the palms of your hands to roll the ball against a smooth surface to make a long dough "snake" about ½ inch thick. Use the butter knife to cut off ½-inch pieces, and then roll each small piece into a ball. Poke the toothpick through each ball to make a hole. Set the beads on a paper towel, and follow the microwave directions on page 34. When they are cool, thread them on a long string to make a bracelet or necklace.

Apple Pomander

This sweet-smelling apple keeps closets and drawers smelling good.

•• WHAT YOU WILL NEED ••

- ▶ 1 perfect apple
- ▶ 1 ounce whole cloves
- ▶ 1 tablespoon cinnamon
- ▶ 1 teaspoon nutmeg
- ▶ 1 teaspoon allspice
- ▶ ⅛ teaspoon ginger
- ▶ 18-inch length of ribbon
- ▶ Bowl and skewer

 Push the stem ends of the cloves into the apple — just close enough to touch. Cover the apple completely with cloves.

 Mix the cinnamon, nutmeg, allspice, and ginger in the bowl. Roll the apple pomander in the spice mixture. Leave the pomander in the bowl in a warm spot for 2 or 3 weeks. Roll it in the spices occasionally to help the apple dry, harden, and shrink.

 Have your grown-up helper pierce the pomander apple lengthwise with the skewer. Thread a double length of ribbon through the top of the pomander. Tie a knot and a bow at the bottom and make a loop for hanging at the top.

Be an Apple Cook

Now that you are an apple artist, it's time to create masterpieces of a different nature — tasty ones! Apples are wonderful to eat right off the tree, but they are also a terrific addition to many recipes. There's much more to cooking with apples than just applesauce!

You can use them for every meal and all the snacks in between. Apples are healthful, sweet, and easy to use, so tie on an apron, grab your grown-up helper by the hand, and head for the kitchen!

Harvest Apple Pie

Everyone's favorite dessert! Now you can help make one of your own.

⋅⋅ WHAT YOU WILL NEED ⋅⋅

- ▶ Pastry for a double 9- or 10-inch pie crust
- ▶ ¼ cup melted apricot jam or marmalade
- ▶ 5 large apples
- ▶ 2 tablespoons lemon juice
- ▶ ½ cup brown sugar, packed
- ▶ 2 tablespoons all-purpose flour.
- ▶ ½ teaspoon cinnamon
- ▶ ¼ teaspoon nutmeg
- ▶ 1 tablespoon butter
- ▶ 1½ teaspoons milk
- ▶ 1 teaspoon sugar

 Turn the oven on to 400°F. "Grease" a 10-inch pie plate.

 Roll out half of the pastry dough and fit it carefully into the pie plate. Brush it with the melted jam. Put the plate in the refrigerator while you prepare the apples.

 Have your grown-up helper peel, core, and cut the apples into small chunks. Put the chunks in a bowl, and sprinkle the lemon juice over them; mix well.

 In another bowl, mix the brown sugar, flour, cinnamon, and nutmeg.

 Get the pie plate with the crust out of the 'fridge, and put half of the apples into it. Sprinkle half of the sugar mixture on top. Add the rest of the apples and then the rest of the sugar. Cut the butter into little pieces and scatter them over the apples.

 Roll out the top crust and place it over the filling. Use a fork to press the edges of the top and bottom crusts together. Cut three little air vents in the middle of the pie so the steam can escape while the pie is cooking.

 Brush the top of the pie with the milk and sprinkle with sugar.

 Place the pie on the middle shelf in the oven and bake it for 50 to 60 minutes. Let the pie cool for at least ten minutes — before serving with ice cream and milk!

Don't Burn the Crust!

If the crust edges brown before the pie is done, cover them with strips of aluminum foil.

Broiled Apple Kabobs

Whether you choose these hot kabobs or the cold variety on page 42,
these are fast, fun finger-food treats! Enjoy these sweet kabobs with your dinner.
They might even count as a vegetable!

•• WHAT YOU WILL NEED ••

- 6 apples
- ¼ cup butter
- ½ teaspoon ground cinnamon
- ½ teaspoon ground nutmeg
- ½ teaspoon ground ginger
- 1 tablespoon smooth peanut butter
- Corer
- Sharp knife
- 6 skewers
- Small pan
- Basting brush

1. Wash and core the apples. Ask a grown-up helper to cut each apple into six wedges, and then cut each wedge in half. There will be twelve pieces from each apple.

2. Put the apples onto the skewers. Push them right to the middle, so they don't fall off while they are cooking!

Apples have been around for 750,000 years!

3. Melt the butter in a small pan. Mix in the cinnamon, nutmeg, ginger, and peanut butter. Stir the mixture until it is smooth and well mixed.

4. Take the basting brush, and carefully brush the hot peanut butter mixture onto the apples. It's a bit like painting a picture. You are making an edible masterpiece!

5. Ask your helper to broil these for 4 minutes and to turn them two or three times while they are broiling. You can help to carefully baste them every time they are turned.

Chilly Apple Kabobs

Enjoy these on a hot afternoon, and try to eat them right away.
If you keep them in the 'fridge, the fruit may brown, but they will still taste great!

WHAT YOU WILL NEED

- 3 apples
- 2 bananas
- 1 large bunch seedless grapes
- 1 pint strawberries
- Yogurt, cinnamon, and granola (optional)
- Corer
- Sharp knife
- Bowls for the fruit
- 6 skewers

then to cut each wedge in half. How many pieces will you get out of each apple? (For the answer, see page 60.)

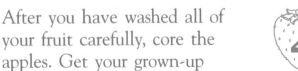 **1** After you have washed all of your fruit carefully, core the apples. Get your grown-up helper to cut them into six wedges,

 2 Peel and slice the bananas into chunks, each about 2 inches wide.

 3 Set up a work station on the table where you will be making the kabobs. Put each fruit into a different bowl.

 4 Starting with the apple chunks, put the fruit on the skewers. Alternate the various fruits, making a pattern of colors and

tastes. Plan ahead so that all the skewers get some of each kind of fruit. Someone would be very sad if he or she didn't get any strawberries on a skewer!

 5 Serve with yogurt, sprinkled with cinnamon and granola.

All apples are green when they are young. You can tell that some apples are ripe and ready to eat when they change from green to red, but some — such as Granny Smiths — remain green even when they are completely ripe.

ABC Bread

(**A**pple-**B**anana-**C**hocolate Chip Bread)
Makes one 8" x 4" loaf

*Do you think you could create a recipe that includes an ingredient starting with every letter in the alphabet? This recipe is as far as I could get, but you should try your luck. Remember, you don't necessarily have to eat the recipe. Use your imagination. **X**ylophone keys and **Z**ippers would be great!*

• • • • • • • • • • • • • • • WHAT YOU WILL NEED • • • • • • • • • • • • • • •

- ▶ 1¾ cups flour
- ▶ 2 teaspoons baking powder
- ▶ ½ teaspoon baking soda
- ▶ 2–3 ripe bananas
- ▶ ½ cup brown sugar
- ▶ ⅓ cup vegetable oil
- ▶ 2 large eggs
- ▶ 1 medium apple

- ▶ ½ cup miniature chocolate chips
- ▶ Butter or margarine
- ▶ A large and a small mixing bowl
- ▶ Wooden spoon
- ▶ Fork
- ▶ Paper towel
- ▶ 8" x 4" loaf baking pan

1 Turn the oven on to 350°F before you start making the bread.

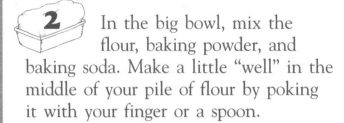 **2** In the big bowl, mix the flour, baking powder, and baking soda. Make a little "well" in the middle of your pile of flour by poking it with your finger or a spoon.

 3 In the smaller bowl, use a fork to mash your bananas. This is the fun part!

 4 Add the sugar, oil, and eggs to the mashed bananas. Beat them in well.

5 Pour this mixture into the well you made in the flour. Mix everything together. Try to get all the lumps out, so your bread is smooth and free from air bubbles.

 6 Ask your helper to dice the apple. Add the apple pieces and the chocolate chips to the batter. Give it a final stir to mix.

7 Put a bit of butter or margarine on a paper towel, and rub it all over the inside of the baking pan. This is called "greasing" the pan, and it keeps the bread from sticking to the sides.

8 Pour the batter into the greased baking pan, put the pan in the hot oven, and bake it for 60 minutes or until it is brown on top and dry on the inside. (Stick a wooden toothpick into it to check.) Make sure you let it cool before you dig in!

Measure carefully! Even when you're only a little off or forget only one ingredient, you can change (and spoil!) the entire recipe.

Applesauce

Makes about 5 cups

The best apples for applesauce are Golden Delicious or Winesap.
Use a few of each and you will have an extra-special snack!

WHAT YOU WILL NEED

- 10–15 apples
- Water
- Sprinkle of cinnamon and sugar
- Sharp knife
- Large saucepan
- Large bowl
- Potato masher
- Apple corer/peeler

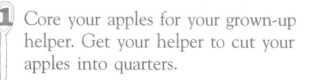 **1** Core your apples for your grown-up helper. Get your helper to cut your apples into quarters.

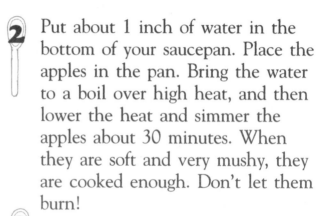 **2** Put about 1 inch of water in the bottom of your saucepan. Place the apples in the pan. Bring the water to a boil over high heat, and then lower the heat and simmer the apples about 30 minutes. When they are soft and very mushy, they are cooked enough. Don't let them burn!

3 Get your helper to drain the apples and put them in a large bowl.

4 Roll up your sleeves and use the potato masher to get mashing! The apples are hot, so try not to splash the mushy apples. Mash until your arms get tired — or until the sauce is the right consistency for you, which might just be at the same time!

5 Sprinkle cinnamon and sugar on top, and enjoy your delicious applesauce warm or cold! Save a little to use in the Applesauce Brownies recipe on page 48.

Easy Blender Applesauce

Makes about 2 to 2½ cups

Don't try this recipe without a grown-up helper to operate the blender.

•• WHAT YOU WILL NEED ••

- ◗ 5 large apples
- ◗ 1 cup water
- ◗ Dash of cinnamon and sugar
- ◗ Blender

Peel, core, and quarter the apples with your helper.

Put a few apple pieces into the blender at a time, and blend with the cup of water.

When all the apples are in, add the cinnamon and sugar, and continue blending until mushy.

Scoop out the sauce and serve in cups — enjoy!

Applesauce Brownies

These should really be called "Brownies That Just Happen to Have Applesauce in Them"! They are very easy to make and more healthful than ordinary brownies, so dig in!

···· WHAT YOU WILL NEED ····

- 4 ounces unsweetened baking chocolate
- ½ cup applesauce
- 4 eggs
- ¼ teaspoon salt
- 2 cups sugar
- 1 teaspoon vanilla extract

- 1 cup all-purpose flour
- 9" x 13" baking pan
- Paper towel and butter
- Heavy saucepan
- Large wooden spoon
- Measuring cup
- Large mixing bowl

1 In a heavy saucepan, melt the chocolate over *very low* heat. Ask for grown-up help for this step. Stir the chocolate while you are heating it, and watch carefully so that it doesn't burn! Let the chocolate cool for about ½ hour.

2 While the chocolate is cooling, get the baking pan ready. Rub about 1 tablespoon of butter over the bottom and sides of the pan. (This is called "greasing the pan.")

3 Preheat the oven to 350°F.

4 Stir the applesauce into the melted chocolate.

 5 Beat the eggs in the mixing bowl.

 6 Add the salt, sugar, and vanilla to the eggs.

 7 Add the chocolate to the egg mixture.

 8 Gently mix the flour into the egg and chocolate mixture.

 9 Pour the batter into the baking pan.

 10 Bake the brownies for about 25 minutes. If you poke them with a wooden toothpick, it should come out dry.

The hardest part of the entire recipe is waiting for the brownies to cool so that you can eat them!

Apple Scramble

Makes 4 small servings

Make a fun breakfast surprise for your family! This recipe is very easy, so you and a big sister or brother can make it for a parent — now that's a treat!

WHAT YOU WILL NEED

- 5 eggs
- 1 tablespoon honey
- 2 apples
- 2 tablespoons butter
- Bread and butter for toast
- Mixing bowl
- Fork
- Grater
- Skillet
- Toaster
- Wooden spoon

1 Carefully crack the eggs into the mixing bowl. If you happen to get a little shell in the bowl, use a big piece of shell as a magnet to scoop the escaped shells out!

2 Beat the eggs with a fork. Add the honey.

 3 Use a grater to grate the apples. Be careful not to "grate" your fingers, and don't get any seeds in the bowl.

4 Get your helper to melt the butter in the skillet over medium heat while you put the toast into the toaster. Add the apple to the egg mixture, and stir with a wooden spoon.

5 Pour the egg mixture into the skillet. Cook and stir the eggs constantly until they are fluffy and dry.

6 Butter the toast and put it on a plate. Serve the eggs on top. Pour yourself (or the person you are treating) a glass of juice and enjoy!

Scrambled Apple Words

Can you unscramble the following groups of letters to make a list of apple words?

REET

SOOMBLS

SHIMCONT

PAPSEELCAU

EDSE

RECOR

OBB

RAGNNY MISHT

CHARRDO

REDIC

For answers, see page 60.

Baked Apple Butter

Makes 8 to 10 half-pints

Although there isn't a drop of butter in this recipe, it tastes great on muffins,
toast, or bread. Or, put it in a pretty dish and give it as a gift.
The butter should be kept in the refrigerator.

•• WHAT YOU WILL NEED ••

- 12 large apples
- 3 cups apple cider
- 4 cups brown sugar
- 2 teaspoons cinnamon
- ½ teaspoon cloves
- ¼ teaspoon nutmeg
- 1 teaspoon allspice
- Corer/peeler
- Sharp knife
- Large pot
- Large casserole dish or dutch oven

1 Core the apples to get them ready for your helper to peel and cut into eighths.

2 Put the apples and the cider into the pot. Put the pot on the stove over medium-high heat, and cook until the liquid is simmering. Cover the pot, lower the heat, and cook the apples until they are soft and mushy. This usually takes between 30 and 60 minutes.

3 Get your helper to pour the apple mush into a large casserole dish or dutch oven.

4 Add the sugar, cinnamon, cloves, nutmeg, and allspice. Stir well.

5 Bake in the oven at 275°F for 1½–2 hours or until the apple butter is dark and thick.

6 Cool the apple butter, and store it in tightly covered jars in the refrigerator.

Candied Carob Apples

Yum! A way of making something good even better!

WHAT YOU WILL NEED

- 8 medium apples
- 1 pound carob chips
- Chopped peanuts (optional)
- Shredded coconut (optional)
- Cookie sheet
- Waxed paper
- 8 wooden popsicle sticks
- Double boiler

1 Wash and dry the apples.

2 Cover the cookie sheet with waxed paper and set it next to the stove.

There are over 300 different varieties of apples!

6 As you finish each one, place it on waxed paper to dry and cool, stick up, while you coat the other apples.

3 Stick popsicle sticks into the stem ends of your apples.

4 With a grown-up helper, melt the carob chips in the top of a double boiler.

5 When the carob is melted, dip the apples, one at a time, into the pot. Swirl them around until they are well coated with the melted carob.

If you like to experiment, sprinkle chopped peanuts or shredded coconut on the apples as soon as they are coated, while the carob is still hot.

Apple-Mint Vinegar

A wonderful, homemade treat that's easy to make!
This can be used as a very special gift.

•• WHAT YOU WILL NEED ••

- 1 cup fresh apple mint leaves from the garden (see page 20)
- 2 cups apple cider vinegar
- Paper towels
- 1 sterilized, large-mouthed glass jar
- Small, decorative glass bottles
- Plastic funnel
- Coffee filter
- Corks

1 Pick some mint leaves — enough to fill 1 cup — and gently wash them. Lay them on paper towels. Cover them with more paper towels. Put them outside on a warm, breezy day. After 2 or 3 hours they will be all ready to use!

2 Combine the vinegar and apple mint leaves in your glass jar. Screw the lid on tightly. If the lid is metal, put a piece of plastic wrap over the jar before you screw the lid on. Leave the jar on the kitchen counter for 3 to 4 weeks. Give it a shake every few days.

3 Hooray! Now you can finish this project! Take your clean, sterilized decorative glass bottle and put the funnel in the top. Next, place a coffee filter in the funnel, and slowly pour the vinegar through. The filter will catch all the pieces of apple mint.

4 Add one clean stalk of apple mint to the vinegar bottle, and put the cork in the top. Label the bottle, and make sure people know that you made it!

Uses for Apple-Mint Vinegar

◆ In mayonnaise or whipped cream for fruit salads

◆ As a marinade for lamb or other meat

◆ With oil for salad dressing

Apple Pizza

WHAT YOU WILL NEED

- 1 cup butter (room temperature)
- ⅔ cup sugar
- 1 egg
- 1 teaspoon vanilla
- 2½ cups sifted all-purpose flour
- ½ teaspoon salt
- 1 tablespoon cinnamon
- Peanut butter
- Red jam (your favorite)
- Ground almonds

- Dried apple slices (see pages 18-19)
- Bowl and wooden spoon
- Plastic wrap
- Paper towel and margarine
- Cookie sheet
- Rolling pin
- Spatula
- Plate, 8 or 9 inches wide
- Butter knife

1 Using a wooden spoon, mix the butter and sugar together in the bowl until they are creamy and smooth. Beat in the eggs and vanilla. Slowly add the flour, salt, and cinnamon. Completely mix the dough until it forms a ball.

2 Cover the dough with plastic wrap, and put the bowl in the refrigerator for 3 or 4 hours, until it is chilled.

3 Grease the cookie sheet, and preheat the oven to 350°F.

4 Sprinkle a little flour on a clean, smooth surface, and roll out the dough using short strokes. If the dough starts to stick to the surface, sprinkle a little more flour under it. Keep rolling until the dough is about ⅜ inch thick. Be patient!

5 Use your plate as a pattern to cut out a circle of dough. With the spatula, lift the "crust" carefully onto the cookie sheet. Make "mini-pizzas" with leftover dough.

6 Bake the cookie crust for about 8-10 minutes, or until the dough is slightly

browned. Cool the crust thoroughly before adding toppings.

7 Spread the cookie crust first with some peanut butter, then add jam "sauce." Arrange the apple slices just the way you want them. Sprinkle the top with the ground almonds.

8 Cut in pizza-style wedges and serve with a glass of cold milk. *Mangia bene!* (which means *eat well* in Italian).

Answer Page

What Is a Metaphor?
(page 9)

"The Big Apple" (New York City)

"Rotten to the core" (something or someone that's bad through and through)

"Polish the apple" (which means "flatter someone")

Apple Puzzle
(page 11)

Down

1. MICHIGAN
2. VIRGINIA
3. NEW YORK
4. PENNSYLVANIA

Across

1. WASHINGTON
2. CALIFORNIA
3. NORTH CAROLINA

Chilly Apple Kabobs
(page 42)

6 x 2 = 12

Scrambled Apple Words
(page 50)

TREE
BLOSSOM
MCINTOSH
APPLESAUCE
SEED
CORER
BOB
GRANNY SMITH
ORCHARD
CIDER